Contents

List of Nutmilks

About the Author

Candia Lea Cole has been creatively involved with food preparation since she began exploring the world of vegetarianism at the age of seventeen.

Candi became keenly interested in "diet reform" when, she says, "after a personal history of ill-health that was ineffectively medicated by prescription drugs, and exacerbated by 'unconscious dietary habits,' there was nowhere else to turn to for help except back to nature."

Embarking on a whole-foods lifestyle, while learning about herbal medicine and wholistic healing principles, finally paved the way to Candi's health and heightened spiritual consciousness.

Candi has since made it her livelihood to develop innovative ways (combining aesthetic, hygienic, ethical, humane, and economic principles) of nourishing the whole body with healing gourmet foods and herbs. Her recipes emphasize the personal and planetary values of preparing foods in a manner that honors creation (the life essence) while being kind to animals and considerate of our agricultural resources.

Candi's professional interests include teaching children, teens, and adults the art and science of preparing health-enhancing cuisine, in addition to the principles of living in tune with nature. She has also managed catering services known as Gourmet Gatherings and Meals That Heal. She lives in Minnesota.

Acknowledgments

I am especially grateful for the supportive friends and acquaintances who have been present for the birth of my dietary ideas, and who have faithfully watched the fruits of my labor grow and ripen, while trusting me to find everything (and more) within myself in order to complete my books.

Those individuals include Gerald Dresow, Louise Frechette and Gary Arnold, Kate Odan O'Keefe, James Reyer, Judith Roska, Mandira Gasal, Faith O' Toole, Rick King, Bonnie Rubenstein Behr and David Behr, Dale Vanderjagt, Stanlee Willhite, Paul Juba, Anne Redpath, Dr. Paul Nash, Hal Brennan, and Mitchell Seidenfeld.

I would also like to express my appreciation to

Jean O'Hern—for seeing me "not for the woman I am, but for the angel I may be," and for her immensely giving friendship.

Marcus Thell—for meals once shared in a nutritious spirit, and for realizing when to let cocoons emerge as self-fulfilled butterflies.

Dr. Richard Barmakian—for his special impact on my health destiny and for introducing me to the beautiful blue-flowering plant, flax.

My mother Barbara—for empowering me with her courage to always be pregnant with ideas ahead of their time.

My (late) father whose "passage" has made every living moment of my life count in a whole new way.

My son Bohdan—for his sweet inspiration, and for his eager tastebuds and young helping hands, which put their stamp of approval on each and every nutmilk.

Daniel Wiemer—for his readiness and willingness to illustrate the essence of my writings in such a delicious way. Dan is a most dedicated Minneapolis artist whose talent only begins to show itself on the cover and pages of my books.

Kathy Hayes—for her nimble fingers and mind, which typed my Greek-to-her manuscripts in record time, so that they could reach their destiny.

Howard Weeks—for receiving my manuscripts in a spirit of openness, and for his warmly human approach to the business of making books for a better world.

Thomas Suttle—for his constant loving companionship, unquestioning devotion, and vigorous support of my life's work, which made it entirely possible for everything to evolve in the perfect nick of time.

From the Author

It was over a decade ago that a spark of inspiration for a "cooks" book, featuring "recipes that heal," wafted into my mind. Now, I welcome the illuminating reality of it.

This moment has surely taken a while to arrive, hasn't it? I'm inclined to believe it was waiting—waiting, that is, for myself—(and perhaps others as well) to grow in awareness of the principles for living healthfully through Nature and her wonderful world of natural foods.

Among my enjoyable moments of creating forty nutmilks, there have been *hundreds* of other meals along the way that I've chosen to envision, taste, serve, and build time to write about. Thus, a much earlier conceived book was "rebirthed" into this "easier to deliver" one, and others yet to come.

I never thought the time so long awaited to share the outcome of my labor with you would seem sweetly insignificant, but it does. What seems most meaningful today is that the interest in wholesome planetary foods shows sunny promise of being here to stay.

I'm thankful for the bits of knowledge I began to glean in yesteryears from the pioneers of the "natural foods" movement, who showed me how a little historical dietary inspiration can go a long way in inventing more of the same.

As my efforts to be inventive with new foods flourish, I'm made more profoundly aware that the food discoveries that each of us can make in our lifetimes will impact humankind for a long time to come. Prodding new awareness, they'll encourage the new kinds of nourishment our evolving bodies, minds, and spirits naturally seek.

As you taste some of the food ideas in my book(s), it is my sincere hope that you will be thoughtfully inspired to seeks ways of broadening your life-long appetites, while nourishing yourself in a creative, natural, and intimate way. Your body deserves the very best care that you alone have the ultimate potential to find and lovingly give it.

I have always considered my own exploration of whole foods the opportunity of a lifetime because it has taught me how to feel healthier, happier, and more intrinsically aware of what a balanced state of being is.

There was a time in my early dietary upbringing when I followed where the culinary path of the 1950s and 1960s led. In my teen years, I found myself complaining about a number of perplexing aches and pains symptomatic of disease. I had no real understanding of how they had culminated until I was introduced to the idea that "we are what we eat." I began to interpret the implications of such, arriving at the all-encompassing conclusion that deficiencies and imbalances in my lifestyle, including my diet of foods (and my "mental diet" of thoughts) had co-created my distressed condition.

With the help of mentors and friends much wiser than I, I was encouraged to take a new kind of responsibility for my health. It was made clear to me that the prescription drugs administered frequently during my youth were more capable of suppressing and compounding my ailments than treating them. Nature, I was informed, contained a vast pharmacy of natural healing agents—namely whole foods and herbs—that I could more safely rely on.

My mother, who had by then become as concerned as I about my past, present, and future nutritional welfare, began to seek out new-fashioned foods, a brave number of informative books on the subject of wholistic healing, and people practicing the rediscovered natural healing arts in an effort to help me recover my health.

Well, the new breed of health practitioners I was bound to visit couldn't promise me instant wellness, and the untrodden land of health food preparation didn't guarantee love at first bite. But I did find myself becoming appreciably hungry for the information being presented to me about food, nutrition, and "natural cures," as I sought clues to the cause of everything I had suffered, from jaundice and gallstones to ovarian cysts.

I knew I was being guided on a path of self-discovery and change as I developed a good habit of chewing on the ideas of several health educating authors such as Greg Brodsky, Adelle Davis, Herbert Shelton, Paavo Airola, Richard Barmakian, and many others. Each provided a meal in itself of exciting nutritional discoveries being made at the time. Eventually, I couldn't resist implementing their empirically tested health practices in my own life.

Perhaps the most valuable insight I gained after months of their revealing application, was that the human body is a miraculously functioning thing! And my own, I figured, deserved more respect than I had ever given it before.

While considering many of my lifelong dietary habits, I realized what a difficult task my body must have had for years whenever I ate haphazardly. What I mean to imply is that I didn't understand my body's nutritional needs, so I couldn't possibly nourish them accordingly.

I found that I had often naively savored foods in incompatible combinations (as many people do) and indulged in them at times of the year when they offered unsuitable kinds of fuel for the body's changing needs, i.e., noninsulating watermelon in the chill of winter, and bulk producing oatmeal in the heat of spring and summer.

As I gradually grew more in tune with the kinds of whole foods that Nature provides in seasonal order for the body to sustain balance and regenerate itself (versus foods that cause imbalance and degeneration), a more loving appreciation of my body and Nature began to take root in me.

I fondly recall the times during my unfolding independent study of health when I would bring a basket filled with a miscellany of natural foods and juices (and an armful of books) outdoors with me to nourish my body and thoughts. My intimate hours spent in Nature's outdoor classroom (one very memorable spring, summer, and autumn semester) served as a catalyst that I credit for directing my life on a whole new course.

Mostly I attribute my breakthrough to the sun's countenance shining upon my newly absorbent mind, the outdoor breezes flooding my lungs with the essence of fresh air (and cosmological energy), and a stomach content to effortlessly digest my picnics. The unmistakable physical energy I was gaining also promoted a mental clarity I had never before experienced. I just couldn't help but feel that the elements of Nature—both gross and subtle—were empowering me to heal myself.

It wasn't long before I began to feel as if Mother Nature herself was gently tapping on my consciousness as if to say to me "I am here to guide you. The life essence encompasses us. It serves us with pure energy. Just as the intelligence of the entire universe fills each cell of the ripened fruits and vegetables I bring you, it can be awakened in your cells as you partake of them. Look to me, for all that your body, mind, and spirit need, for I function intrinsically through a Creator who has made certain that you are provided everything you could ever want to be peaceful and feel well."

Gradually the cloudy feeling that had lingered around me for many years (in which I felt separate or alone) and the feelings of powerlessness to overcome my limitations began to disperse. It became crystal clear to me that Nature was a powerfully healing friend of mine (and anyone else who cared to live interdependently with her).

The life-enhancing lesson I was learning was that "Nature lives to serve." I began to realize how we can all bring harmony to one another (and not just absent mindedly coexist) when we seek her gifts and use their healing energies to help ourselves and the planet.

Eager to bring more harmony to the earth, I fathomed the importance of my maintaining a higher level of personal energy that would sustain my physical actions while continuing to make my spirit more apparent to me.

Since my growing experience was showing me that fruits, vegetables, grains, nuts, and seeds were the easiest foods for the body to assimilate and transform into energy, I knew the energy at my command would continue to increase as I upleveled my eating experience. I also gathered that as I purified both my physical and mental bodily functions through a diet of pure foods, pure thoughts, and self-love I could reach my true health potential.

As time went on, I proved this to myself in a profound way. One day I knew—in my mind and heart—that sickness would never have to be a part of my life again as long as I lived with a cooperative spirit of personal and planetary affinity. A new found freedom and peace filled me.

In retrospect, I know that this special understanding came to me at a time when I needed it most. For my

ailing body and mind, and my slumbering spirit, had for
many years been "wholistically yearning" to know that
I was more than that experience alone. My whole being
was seeking its natural strength and balance and its
God-given right to health and wholeness. Thankfully,
it found some of each.

Today I consider my passing health trials a rich
blessing as they continue to serve a brilliant function in
my infinitely healing life. I continue to seek the gifts of
the earth, gathering ancient and new relics of foods and
herbs together in a spirit of innovation and regeneration.
The wondrous power that Nature has to create awareness
and meet the body and mind's ever-changing needs is
awesome.

I hope you will join me in an abundant spirit of
believing we can create planetary health in our lifetime,
by living in tune with the life essence.

Paraphrasing one of my favorite quotes

> "What you are is God's gift to you. . . . What
> you are becoming is your gift to God."

May I add, God's gifts to us are the flowers, fruits, and
trees. Our gift to God is what we affectionately create for
ourselves and humanity with those flowers, their sweet
nectar, and the fruit of the trees.

Bountiful blessings!

Candi

Once you discover the possibilities for creating a whole new foodstyle, you can discover the possibilities for creating a whole new you!

Not Milk . . .
Nutmilks!

- *You cannot digest milk because you have a lactose intolerance?*

- *You prefer not to drink milk because of the antibiotics and growth hormones it contains?*

- *You are a vegetarian and would rather not drink milk drawn from animals by methods less than humane?*

Not Milk . . .

With today's kaleidoscopic focus on healthy dietary lifestyles, and the colorful myriad of food options that can be explored in the process of attaining one, I have a smiling hunch that those of you who've picked up this book are seekers.

Chances are your dietary interests are special and you want your food choices to match. Well, if I may say so, "You've come to the right book!"

If you have made the choice to not drink milk, or if you're simply becoming inclined to phase milk out of your menus, the forty enthusiastically developed recipes herein ought to ease you on your culinary way.

I hear more voices these days declaring healthful and humane reasons for quenching their thirst with extra tumblers of fresh juices, herbal teas, and dairy imposters versus the so-called "real thing" floating in waxed cartons. Whether or not your premises for deciding to elude such a popular beverage first originated in your alimentary tract or your brain, you have, according to the ongoing newscasts reporting on modern-day milk production, made a choice that will add years to your life.

The perilous effect of what comes from a mechanically squeezed udder is not entirely new "news." But it seems that it has taken a long time for an emotionally clinging public to validate and accept this information. If you are one of the countless individuals who has always fondly remembered milk as Nature's ideal sustenance, may I offer a simplistic commentary?

Milk, the way it once was (natural, wholesome, and unprocessed) and the way it is now (unnatural and over processed) have only one admirable characteristic in common—they are both white. However, one of those precious opaque colored liquids is virtuously capable of bringing health to the body, and the other, sicknesses. If, like me, you have resolved to keep cows milk (at least from the good old days) alive in your memory while saying grace at the dining table for the innovation of health-giving alternatives, I have a feeling we are both thinking about building a generation of more deserving nutritional ways.

Nowadays, it is more acceptable than ever before (if not a harmless touch elitist) to know precisely which eatables and drinkables do your body, mind, and emotions good. Furthermore, it is becoming downright respectable to know how the methods employed in producing the food you eat and serve can affect the well-being of our livestock, food acreage, agricultural resources, and economy.

Oftentimes I wish such issues had been more ripe for discussion during my own changing foodstyles, when the idea of sitting down to a cup of nondairy milk was practically unheard of.

It wasn't that I didn't have the pleasure of enough mealtime companions to share brunch with, but few to none of them could stop trying to convince themselves and me that "everybody" needs milk.

In my own small voice I began telling them about the "golden Guernsey" I (and an emerging handful of others) knew was not doing well, even though the dairy industry was. However, they only listened while they gulped, and I

managed to become more unsettled about the milky
moustache shading their lips. Its guise covered for my
new-found facts that it was an artificially inseminated
"solution" of hormones, chemicals, DDT, fungicides,
defoliants, and radioactive fallout (Strontium 90).[1] So
much for blue sky and green pastures.

For any among you who have not heard or read about
the modern-day preparation of milk, you may want to
"imagine" the way in which as many as 100 cows are
injected with the reproductive semen of only a few bulls.
The bulls used in this practice are often reputed to be
hurculean-sized animals that are mated with hormone-
grown "super cows" in order to produce a grossly oversized
milk sac that, more often than not, develops infections
near the cows' teats. Farmers prevent this rather
insufferable condition (which for them amounts to a
diversion of industry time and dollars) by inoculating
livestock feed with penicillin, bactracin, and other
dangerous drugs. Unfortunately the farmers' savings
threaten us as consumers since antibiotics are purported to
have an immune-suppressing function when swallowed
meal upon meal, year after year.

I realized this myself after sixteen years of drinking
milk and eating milk products, when I began to explore
some of my physical complaints with a nutritionist. The
sinusitis, allergies, respiratory weakness, and ovarian cysts
I had long suffered were linked to a deluge of scientific
research in which milk was found to lay the groundwork
for many such diseases. I was as surprised as many
individuals are when first informed that over 45 million
people in the United States alone visit diagnostic clinics
each year to receive treatment for symptoms of dairy borne

---

[1]These contaminants settle in the thyroid gland (particularly in children)
enabling cancers to develop. Paavo Airola, *How To Get Well*, 174.

allergies such as hay fever, eczema, asthma, and lactose intolerance (the inability to digest milk sugar). What came as an even bigger shock to me was the fact that heart disease (the *leading* cause of deaths in the United States) was linked to excessive commercial dairy product consumption—as were digestive disorders, glandular disturbances, arthritis, allergies, cavities, and more! Needless to say, I was alarmingly persuaded then, and remain healthfully convinced now, that my body (amongst others) is considerably better off without the liquid contents of cartons found in every refrigerated grocer's department in the country.

Occasionally, over the years, I have broken my rule of dietary conduct and indulged in some nicely chilled sips of raw goats milk, with the understanding that it is not milk (in and of itself) that causes the body such dietary stress; rather it is the *unnatural preparation* of it.

The famous (late) Dr. Paavo Airola, a worldwide exponent of dietary principles for healthy living, substantiates this fact in his bestselling book *How to Get Well*. In relating his lifelong diary of other foodstyle cultures in such countries as Bulgaria, Armenia, Russia, and Scandinavia, Dr. Airola noted that traditionally heavy milk drinkers were healthy and long-lived. The reasons? Such milk products were not processed by homogenization and pasteurization. According to several other health contemporaries in the United States, the most serious threat in drinking milk lies in the fact that its natural chemical structure is altered by the heat and pressure used in processing to the point of making it indigestible.

Nationally known health authority Dr. Kurt Oster* contends that homogenized and pasteurized milk, which uses extreme heat and pressure to break down the normal sized fat particles (so that cream doesn't separate), causes an enzyme called *xanthine oxidase* (XO) to enter the

*Former chief of cardiology at Park City Hospital, Bridgeport, Connecticut.

bloodstream, which in turn destroys vital body chemicals that normally protect the arteries of the heart.[2]

Why, you may wonder, is milk still the daily choice of the general population if it poses so many serious nutritional problems? The obvious answer I see is that milk continues to be cleverly promoted by the American Dairy Association. Their advertising "magic," including singing radio broadcasts and seductive television commercials, have charmed us with the notion that "everybody needs milk," "milk does a body good," and every "baby" needs milk, so "baby yourself" a little.

After all of this, it is not exactly easy to tell a child or relative (who argues they are just trying to satisfy the requirements of the "basic four" food groups) that the liquid that makes their cereal go snap, crackle, 'n' pop at dawn and washes their cookie down at dusk is not very good for them. However, something I have proved to myself and to my own extended family circle is that it is well worth the effort to try to educate others. Enlightening conversation never hurt anyone's health and well-being. And, if you remember your place (you're not there to take anybody's milk away from them), they just may "wean" themselves.

A kiss of concern, coupled with a refreshingly chilled or cozily warmed glass of nondairy milk in their favorite flavor, may have them all in favor of the satisfying alternative—nutmilks.

Nutmilks, I have discovered, are an excellent replacement for hazardous-to-your-health dairy products, as well as being ideal, low-allergenic replacements for other nondairy milks. I couldn't be more pleased to introduce you to my "thought for food" on preparing them.

[2] "Super Health," by Dr. Kurt Donsbach Ph.D. "Hypoglycemia, Your Bondage or Your Freedom," By Dr. Richard Barmakian, N. D.

. . . Nutmilks!

When you think of nuts, if you think of crunchy, salty appetizers fit for party trays and snacks, it may stretch your imagination to think of the many ways that nuts can be used to create smooth-sipping beverages such as "Banana Walnut 'milk'" or "Apricot Almond Orange 'milk'." Yet, if you can envision the fragrant and flowery orchards in which fresh organic nuts and fruits flourish, your senses may be enchanted by the natural realm of colors, flavors and wholesome nourishment that nutmilks provide.

Like homemade soymilk, which is prepared basically from whole soybeans, and rice milk, prepared from kernels of rice, nutmilk is prepared from whole, shelled nuts. But unlike the preparation of homemade soymilk and rice milk which can take hours, nutmilks can be prepared in as little as 10-15 minutes!

Of course, commercially prepared soy and rice milks are now available to save you the fuss of preparing your own, but you may find, as I have, that commercially prepared nutmilks leave something to be desired. For example, some prepackaged nutmilks are simply dry preparations containing ground nuts sans any spices or flavorings. Since you can easily grind your own nuts at home, these ready-made items are not very cost effective. As for the one or two homogenized nutmilks I've seen on the market, what they gain in terms of convenience they seem to lose in terms of diverse flavors and health benefits.

It is easy and fun to create low-cost homemade
nutmilks that are pleasing to the eye, mind and palate and
rich in nutritional elements. I have always thought that the
actual procedure for turning nuts into nutmilks involves a
bit of alchemy or magic. It's really about blending very
basic, nutritious ingredients into "something better." For
instance, instead of blending nutmilks from just plain nuts
and water, I like to blend nuts with flaxseed, lecithin
granules, accents of fruit, flavoring extracts and a variety of
liquids and wholesome sweeteners, depending on the taste
and nutritional delights I wish to create.

To make the task for preparing nutmilks as simple as
possible, you'll want to dedicate an area of the countertop
in your kitchen as a space where you can fit a blender and
a coffee bean grinder side by side. You will also want easy
access to a one-quart pot and a hand-held strainer. You can
find mesh strainers at any hardware store or department
store that sells small kitchen appliances.

If you don't have any small containers handy in which
to store a few varieties of nuts, seeds and dried fruits, you
may also want to round up a few decorative glass or
ceramic jars. Once you have the basic tools you need to
blend your ingredients effectively, you can begin to explore
the many whole-food ingredients that lend nutmilks a
unique character.

You may discover, as I have, that the many ingredients
that can be used in creating nutmilks have different "per-
sonalities." Rice syrup, for example, a delicious sweetening
option (made from rice), has a slightly different essence or
"personality" than honey, which is gathered by bees.
Likewise, almonds have an appeal different from that of
walnuts, cashews or pumpkin seeds.

Making a nutmilk, it occurs to me, is a lot like making
a fashion statement. Just as you might choose a "feel good"

blend of colors and fibers from your personal wardrobe to create an expression of you, you could blend the ingredients in your "pantry" to create an expression of your tastes and your relationship with the natural world of whole foods.

All in all, I hope you will enjoy the artistic process for creating nutmilks, as well as the healthy and humane path of culinary innovation they offer you!

Food
For Thought

Nature's Pantry of Nutmilk Ingredients

Nuts and Seeds

Nuts

Nuts are the hard-shelled dry fruits or seeds of several kinds of plants, usually trees. Some readily available nuts suitable for nutmilk preparation are almonds, cashews, pecans, and walnuts. The soft inner part of the nut is called the *meat* or *kernel*, and the outer covering is called the *shell*. Nuts are a concentrated source of protein, unsaturated fat, the B complex vitamins, vitamin E, calcium, iron, potassium, magnesium, phosphorous, and copper.

Seeds

Seeds are the ripened ovules of plants. Edible seeds such as sesame, sunflower, pumpkin, and pine nuts are rich in protein. They also contain the B complex vitamins; vitamins A, D, and E; phosphorous; calcium; iron; flourine; iodine; potassium; magnesium; zinc; unsaturated fatty acids; and protein. Sesame seeds are particularly rich in calcium content, and sunflower seeds contain fifty percent protein.

The latest nutritional research shows that nuts and seeds, which are rich in essential fatty acids, can actually help the body burn unwanted fat. (See Page 47.)

Good Nuts Make Good Nutmilks

Before you rev up your kitchen blender and get ready to create some marvelous sipping sensations, you'll want to do what most good chefs do when setting out to prepare gourmet cuisine: Make a trip to some of the best whole-foods markets in your town, searching out the best possible selection of fresh nuts and seeds. A nutmilk made from fresh nuts is delightful, but a nutmilk made from anything less than fresh nuts can be a disappointment. That's because nuts contain precious oils which can easily go rancid. Once they go rancid, their flavors get stale or soapy-tasting.

Here are some tips for selecting nuts at the market:

Supermarket Brands of Nuts

These nuts are packaged in see-through cellophane bags and stacked along racks in the supermarket aisles that house baking goods. They often remain on the shelves too long under the glare of fluorescent lighting, which tends to hasten their rancidity. There is also the likelihood that these nuts have been grown with pesticides or fumigants and processed (shelled) with lye. For nutmilks, I do not recommend supermarket nuts.

Whole Foods Coop (or Health Food Store) Brands of Nuts

Nuts found at a whole-foods coop are usually stored in see-through bins, that allow you, the customer, to reach in with a scoop and take out what you need. The freshness of these nuts is largely determined by how fresh the nuts were at the time the wholesaler delivered them to the store and by the length of time they remain in the bins until sold. Stores with a large number of customers and a high turnover of stock are more likely to have a fresher supply. Since the nuts at the coop may or may not be organically raised, you may want to ask a clerk. If you can avoid pesticides on the nuts you use in your nutmilks, by all means do so!

Some health food stores may have an even fresher supply of nuts since they generally don't deal with big bulk and can often afford to refrigerate the nuts they sell. I recommend using discernment when buying nuts at co-ops and health food stores.

Mail Order Supply Company Brands of Nuts

Nuts found through mail order supply companies are perhaps the best source of fresh nuts available. They usually can be counted on to keep nuts refrigerated up until the time they are shipped. I rely on at least a couple of companies who market fresh, raw, organic nuts that have been grown in the rainforest or other healthy ecosystems. By purchasing organically raised nuts, we can help protect the trees and shrubs which maintain the ecosystem. Although they are a little higher priced than commercial nuts, they offer superior flavor, texture and nutrients.

Organic nuts reflect the true costs of growing food in harmony with nature. Nuts grown with chemicals may be cheaper to buy, but the price you pay at the checkout lane doesn't include the price you may expect to pay later, for poisoning the land, poisoning your body, etc.

Two organic suppliers that I sometimes rely on for fresh nuts and seeds are:

Walnut Acres Organic Farms, Penns Creek, PA 17862
1-800 433-3998
Diamond Organics, Freedom, CA 95019
1-888-674-2642

Keeping Nuts and Seeds Fresh

Nuts and seeds, if relatively fresh when purchased, will keep in the refrigerator for approximately four weeks and up to six weeks in the freezer. After purchasing nuts and seeds, simply remove them from their tote bags, transfer them to air-tight glass jars and place in cold storage. Nut butters (the creamy version of nuts) keep for three to four weeks in the refrigerator and up to three months in the freezer.

Nuts Won't Make You Fat, but They May Lower Your Cholesterol

If you're saying to yourself, "Never mind the information about perishable nuts, I want to know if nutmilks will raise my cholesterol or cause me to gain weight,"... I have a reassuring answer for you. "They will do neither!" In fact, all of my nutmilk recipes have zero cholesterol and despite the creamy texture of some, have less then 175 calories* per eight-ounce serving. What nutmilks do have in abundance is something most people have a deficiency of: essential fatty acids. The reason most people are deficient in fatty acids is that these acids are processed out of the food supply.

According to health experts, fatty acids aid the body in growth, tissue repair, hormone regulation and overall immunity. They can also burn unwanted fat and discourage the buildup of arterial plaque caused by foods (including dairy products) that contain saturated fat. In a landmark study conducted at Loma Linda University in California, researchers determined that individuals who ate 2½ ounces of walnuts five or more days a week, lowered their cholesterol by 12 percent!

*7-11 grams of unsaturated fat

"What is important to health is the type of fat we eat," says Walter Willet, chairman of the Department of Nutrition at Harvard University School of Public Health. "People need to realize that some fats are very beneficial. Unsaturated fats, such as those in nuts, seeds and oils, need to be individually ranked, not lumped together with the unhealthy saturated fats."

Food for Thought

If you eat a small serving of nuts for a snack, lunch on a piece of bread spread with nut butter, or sprinkle your favorite salad with sunflower seeds, you have built into your diet a healthy source of calories which are made up of both protein and fat. When you include nutmilks in your diet, you do the same. Drinking a cup of nutmilk is like eating a few fresh nuts out of your hand. Unlike a high-fat milkshake, loaded with saturated fat and, in many instances, hard-to-digest milk proteins, nutmilks are prepared from small amounts of nuts (1/3–1/2 cup per recipe) which are easy to digest.

Calcium Minus the Cow

One of the most common concerns people have when substituting cow's milk with nutmilks, is whether or not nutmilks will provide the body with enough calcium. Rather than serving as a complete replacement for calcium, nutmilks should be thought of as a nutritious calcium supplement.

There are many foods one can eat to boost the body's calcium reserves, including: legumes, tofu, oranges, sea vegetables, miso, and greens such as bok choy and broccoli. In addition to these foods, the nuts and fruits featured in my nutmilk recipes are wonderful sources of calcium, especially almonds, pecans, sesame seeds, sunflower seeds, flaxseed, dried apricots, figs and dates.

Compared with a 7-ounce serving of cow's milk (which has roughly 250 mg. calcium), the calcium content of nutmilk (25-150 mg. depending on the ingredients used) may not seem that impressive.

But only a percentage of the calcium we eat is absorbed well by the body. In fact, according to many health experts, the more dairy products we consume, the more calcium we stand to lose, regardless of how much calcium we take in!

In his book, *Diet for a New America*, John Robbins explains why. "If the diet contains a lot of acid-forming foods (primarily animal foods), then the body in its wisdom withdraws calcium from the bones to balance the pH of the blood."

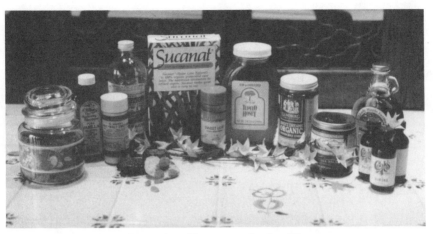

Natural sweeteners also add nutritional value. This tasty array is available at your local coop or health food store.

Options for Sweetening Nutmilks

The following ingredients can be used alone or interchangeably to sweeten your drinks and give them the desired health value you are seeking.

Barley Malt Powder

A natural sweetener, and a fine choice for sweetening nutmilks of all flavors, barley malt powder is derived from grains that have been sprouted, dried, and cooked down to a dry natural malt. "Dr. Bronner's" (brand name) barley malt powder contains a uniquely sweet blend of barley malt, orange juice solids, calcium-magnesium-phosphate, parsley, chia seeds, vegetable protein, dulse, sea lettuce, lemon juice solids, potassium salt, rosehips, anise, and mint.

One part barley malt replaces twenty parts sugar. A dash has only three calories and substitutes for two teaspoons of sugar, giving you a reduction of up to ninety-eight percent of the usual calories without sacrificing sweetness!

Barley malt powder can be used in place of or along with liquid sweeteners. This way, you can reduce the amount of liquid sweeteners and stretch the flavor you desire.

Stevia Rebaudiana (Sweet Leaf) Powder

Stevia is an herbal sweetener, derived from a small herbaceous shrub grown in Brazil and Argentina and now in the southwestern United States. If you are on a low-sugar, low-carbohydrate, or weight-loss diet, stevia is an ingredient you will want to look into. Stevia's sweetening power is thirty to eighty times that of sugar, yet it has only one calorie per ten leaves. It can be used in the same way as barley malt powder. A pinch per cup of liquid will do.

Sweet leaf's licoricelike taste best complements nutmilks that have a minty, carob, or pumpkin flavor.

South American Indians have used this sweetener for centuries, and, although it is just becoming popular in the United States, Japanese researchers have found it to have many healthful qualities, including (1) beneficial regulating effects on blood sugar; (2) inhibitory effects on bacteria in the mouth (which aid in preventing tooth decay);
(3) tonifying effects that counteract fatigue; and (4) regulating effects on metabolic functions, including diuretic properties that aid weight loss.

Stevia also contains antibacterial, antiyeast, and antifungal properties.

Honey

Because of its taste, texture, and overall availability, honey is an ingredient used in many of the nutmilk recipes herein.

Honey varies in texture, flavor, and color, depending upon the types of flowers from which the nectar is gathered. As a rule, dark honeys are nutritionally superior to light honeys, although they impart a stronger flavor.

Since honey is almost twice as sweet as cane sugar, smaller amounts of it are needed for sweetening purposes.

Unfiltered raw honey contains large amounts of carbohydrates in the form of sugars, small amounts of minerals, and B complex vitamins, as well as vitamins C, D, and E.

Nutmilk recipes generally call for approximately two tablespoons of honey per quart of nutmilk. However, this amount can be adjusted to suit your needs. Less can be used with a dash of barley malt powder or stevia powder.

Maple Syrup

Good quality maple syrup (such as some authentic Canadian and Vermont versions, as well as syrup from small producers) can serve as a delicious addition to nutmilks. Although it is not particularly abundant in nutritional value, it does contain sugars, which, when used in moderation, can furnish quick energy to the body. Maple flavored extract can be used along with a lesser quantity of the syrup to impart a richer flavor. Make certain the syrup you use does not contain salt, chemical preservatives, defoaming agents, or formaldehyde (from the pellets used to tap the trees).

Brown Rice Syrup

This is a delectable liquid sweetener, pale blonde in color, resembling honey in texture and taste appeal. Rice syrup is made from organic brown rice. It is first ground into a meal, then cooked, before natural cereal enzymes are added—which convert the starches in the rice to relatively complex natural sugars. A sweet liquid is squeezed from the mixture and cooked briefly until it thickens. This is truly a nutritious sweetener, since the body does not need to release extra insulin in order to break down the *maltose* (malted grain). Its light flavor is particularly delightful in nutmilks containing fruit.

Molasses

This is a thick syrup (light to dark brown in color) having a distinctive flavor ranging from mellow to strong.

Blackstrap molasses is the residue left after the last possible extraction of sugar from cane or beet. While it contains many nutrients, it also contains residues from the sugar growing and refining process.

Unsulphured, golden molasses (also known as West Indies Barbados molasses) is less nutritionally rich than blackstrap molasses, but it does not contain residues and is a more pleasant-tasting way to obtain iron, calcium, and traces of other vitamins and minerals.

I do not usually use molasses to flavor nutmilks, since even the golden variety imparts a strong flavor. However, it is a nutritious option.

Sucanat

Sucanat is the trade name given to a 100 percent organic granulated sugarcane juice that adds nourishment to nutmilks. Unrefined, it is considered to be a healthy alternative to refined sugar. Sucanat supplies sweet-tasting, easy-to-use calcium, phosphorus, potassium, chromium, magnesium, iron, and vitamins A and C.

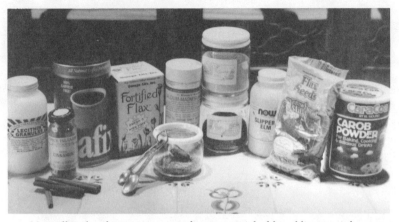

Nutmilks, already nutritious, may be super-enriched by adding special ingredients that are available at most food coops and health food stores.

Ingredients that Fortify Nutmilks

Flaxseeds

Flaxseeds are a key ingredient of nutmilks, providing fabulous food value and fiber. They are derived from the lovely blue flowering flaxseed plant that grows in the summer and is widely cultivated in the northern United States, Canada, and Europe.

Flax is a multipurpose herb, also known as *linseed*. Fiber from the stalks, along with the oil and mucilage from the seeds, have been used for centuries by weavers, painters, and beauticians as well as herbalists and cooks.

The seeds, which are chocolate brown in color, can be found at most co-ops and health food stores. The latter is likely to stock an enriched variety called Fortified Flax, made by OmegaLife, Inc. This brand assures you of an organically grown product rich in various nutritional cofactors, and minerals which aid in the effectiveness of its assimilation. Also rich in soluable fiber, flax is quite capable of replacing laxative products such as Metamucel.

Last, but not least, flaxseed contains an ingredient called *Omega* 3 which is effective in the medical treatment of various degenerative diseases in this country. Omega 3 is an essential fatty acid *(linolenic acid)* that often becomes lost in food processing. Essential to a preventative diet in the 1980s and 1990s, it is known by researchers to reduce serum tryglycerides, or "hard trans fats" as they are often called. These hard fats cannot be used as an energy source by the body as the body is unable to digest them properly.

The most noticeable effect of hard trans fats on the body is the appearance of cellulite. Hidden trans fats lodge in other areas of the body as well, such as the liver and heart, causing hardening of the liver, atherosclerosis, etc. Milk fat (from pasteurized milk) is said to contain two to eight percent trans fats that the body is ill equipped to metabolize.

Until the discovery of Omega 3's effect on the dislodging of fats from the body, it seemed there was no answer to this problem. Now, however, researchers are finding that one to three tablespoons of flax in one's daily diet can help to overcome dry skin, cellulite, constipation, colitis, ulcers, hypoglycemia, diabetes, heart disease, cholesterol, calcium deficiencies, and reproductive and immune system related disorders in a matter of a few weeks or months.[1] These nutritional discoveries certainly encouraged my culinary discoveries!

For nutmilk recipes, you'll want to experiment with one level tablespoon of ground flaxseed per quart of milk. Your task in making flax an effective ingredient in the drinks will be to first grind the seeds in an electric seed grinder until they become a fine powder. Once mixed with the other ingredients (including water), they will release a

[1]Unsaturated fatty acids combine with vitamin D in the body in order to make calcium available to the tissues.

mucilage that creates body and nutritional bulk. Since flaxseeds have a fibrous outer husk, you will most likely want to strain your drinks before sipping.

Lecithin

A valuable ingredient in nutmilk preparation, lecithin is a food supplement extracted from the soybean. It is an emulsifier of fats, and when combined with nuts (which are rich in fatty acids) it enhances their palatability* and aids digestion. You will find that the addition of only one teaspoon of lecithin granules per quart of nutmilk binds the ingredients, making a creamier drink.

Nutritionally speaking, lecithin plays an important part in maintaining a healthy nervous system. A natural constituent of every cell in the human body, lecithin is found in the *myelin sheath*, a fatty protective covering for the nerves. Lecithin is also known for breaking up cholesterol deposits on the arterial walls, helping to prevent heart diseases. Other reported benefits you may experience by adding lecithin to your diet include weight loss, memory improvement, and liver and kidney cleansing. Always keep lecithin granules refrigerated.

Slippery Elm Powder

Slippery elm powder is a delicious and healing herblike food used to fortify nutmilks. It is derived from the inner bark of the deciduous slippery elm tree which is grown and cultivated in North America.

Slippery elm powder has a light and fluffy texture, is pale beige in color, and may remind you of a protein powder with a maplelike aromatic quality. Although it is uncharacteristic of other dairy-, soy-, and egg-rich protein conglomerates, its food value is remarkable.

Slippery elm is as nutritious as oatmeal and possesses

---

*Liquid lecithin is not advisable for use in nutmilks as it alters the taste. Use the fresh granules instead.

many enzymes that aid the body's digestive processes. Its mucilage content is soothing and healing to ailments such as coughs, catarrh, stomach and bowel troubles, and urinary tract irritations. It is an ideal first food for babies or convalescing persons since it is so easy to digest. A healthy measure of slippery elm in a banana- , maple- , or carob-flavored nutmilk will enhance its flavor nicely as well as add texture and nutriment.

Guar Gum

Guar gum is an ingredient that can be used for thickening and fortifying nutmilks. Derived from a plant known as the cluster bean, it is actually a polysaccharide. In some instances you could use it in place of flaxseed.

Guar gum is useful as a dietary aid for intestinal and colon cleansing. It has also been found to help lower serum cholesterol levels.

Capsules of guar gum can be obtained at most health food stores. Each capsule contains roughly 500 mg. of guar gum. You could add anywhere from 2-6 capsules to a recipe depending on the desired thickness.

You may or may not want to strain the beverage afterwards.

Special Extras

Food Flavoring Extracts

Natural nonimitation food flavorings made from the oils of natural herbs, vegetables, and fruits are available at many natural food stores. The concentrated flavoring agents contain no sugar or salt. Look for *Cook's Choice* and Frontier brands that are likely to offer a selection of orange, banana, lemon, almond, vanilla, cinnamon, coconut, butterscotch, cherry, and pineapple.*

Spices

Some of the delightful spices I use for nutmilks include cinnamon, coriander, allspice, nutmeg, mint, and anise. Spices have a long and unique history. They also have medicinal values too important to overlook. To give you an idea, cinnamon is recommended by herbalists for aiding digestion. Recent studies by Japanese researchers show that cinnamon also contains a substance that acts on certain fungi, bacteria, parasites, and botulinus. Other findings suggest other medicinal uses for cinnamon.

Anise and coriander seeds (ground) offer a pleasant-tasting way to soothe an upset stomach, aid digestion, and relieve gas.

Mint will relieve indigestion, colic, and gas and is valuable in a variety of health conditions from fevers and flu to colds, cramps, insomnia, bad breath, and abdominal pains.

Dried Fruits (Unsulfured Varieties)

A variety of dried fruits may be reconstituted for use in nutmilk recipes, and you will find that they lend nutribody to the recipes as well as unique flavors. Try apples,

*The amount of flavoring extracts in a recipe may vary, depending on the strength of the brand used.

apricots, pears, raisins, and unsulphured dates. Dried
fruits contain concentrated natural fruit sugars and
minerals including iron, potassium, phosphorus, and
calcium.

Carob Powder

Carob powder is a sweet and delicious chocolatelike
powder from the fruit (pod) of an evergreen tree
indigenous to the Mediterranean region. Used in
nutmilks, it is a satisfying substitute for cocoa powder,
which contains caffeine and other stimulants. Carob
contains a fair share of protein, natural sugar, calcium,
phosphorus, minerals, and B vitamins.

Cafix Cereal Grain Beverage Powder

Cafix is the name given to a product on the market that
resembles instant coffee. Its caffeine-free, nonaddictive
ingredients include mineral-rich roasted barley, rye,
chicory, and shredded beet roots. Its rich flavor will "wake
you" in the morning without causing sleeplessness at
night. One cup of Cafix contains only seven calories. You
will want to try mixing one to three teaspoons into a
blender of carob-mint nutmilk for a mochalike flavor!

Culinary Helpers

Nutmilk Preparation

Culinary Helpers

Here is what you will need to make nutmilk preparation a snap:

Blender—standard size, high speed model (such as Oster, Waring, Sunbeam, etc.)

Electric seed or coffee bean grinder* (such as Krups, Braun, Oster, Sunbeam, or Moulinex)

Glass, enamel, or stainless one-to-two quart stove pot.

Fine mesh strainer, 4-6″ in diameter, and stirring spoon.

Easy access refrigerator jars and pantry containers for all fresh dry nuts, seeds, spices, nut butters, sweeteners, dried fruits, and flavoring extracts.

*Consider an electric seed grinder one of the most valuable small investments you will make in a kitchen appliance. (They retail for under $20.) I wouldn't consider making nutmilks without one since it saves time in grinding nuts and seeds to the fine consistency needed for smooth, creamy drinks.

Preparing Nutmilks in Five Easy Steps

❶ In a one-quart saucepan, heat 3-4 cups of water. If using juice or other liquids to accent your recipe, you don't need to heat them; simply heat the portion of water you choose to use and add the other liquids.

❷ Using a coffee bean grinder, grind your choice of nuts. To activate grinding blades, simply press down firmly on the cap that covers the grinding unit. If your grinder has a small grinding cup, you may not be able to fit all the nuts in at once. If you can't grind all of the nuts finely, without taxing the motor of the unit, do two separate batches. Some nuts (almonds) will grind up like powder; nuts with a higher oil content (walnuts) may be slightly pasty with a few small unground bits. It's okay to have a few small unground bits, as long as most of the nuts are well ground.

Transfer your ground-up nuts to the blender. Repeat the grinding process, using flaxseed, and transfer them to your blender as well. You'll want to use caution if you sweep the nuts from the unit with your finger—the blades are semi-sharp!

❸ To your blender (which now contains ground nuts), add lecithin granules, the sweetener of your choice, spices and flavoring extract, and fresh or rehydrated fruit, if specified.

❹ Using a glass measuring cup, scoop 1/3 cup water from your saucepan and add to your blender, or 1/2 cup if your recipe features fruit. Using this small amount of water to begin the blending process, helps the ingredients to become cohesive. After about 15 seconds of blending these ingredients into a saucy or pudding like consistency, slowly add the remaining liquid and then blend on high speed for another 15 seconds or longer.

❺ Using a small mixing bowl with a hand-held strainer resting over the top, pour one cup of liquid at a time into strainer. Stir the milk as it goes through the strainer until pulp shows in the strainer. Press any remaining liquid through strainer. Repeat until you have emptied the blender. This should take only a couple of minutes. To store nutmilk, pour contents of blender into air-tight quart-sized bottles and keep refrigerated for up to three days. Since nutmilks are a four season beverage, you can drink them chilled or warmed.

Helpful Hints for Nutmilk Preparation

• Is straining nutmilks necessary? Although it is a matter of preference, straining nutmilks will give them the mouth appeal of milk or cream versus a semi-fibery drink whose ingredients may separate if left in the refrigerator. I like to strain nutmilks (using a relatively fine mesh strainer) when serving friends or guests.

• What can I do with leftover nut and flaxseed hulls accumulated during the straining process? Mix food pulp into baked goods. Flaxseed gives a hearty, moist quality to cakes, muffins, etc.

• What if my nutmilk is too thick to pour through the strainer? Simply reduce the amount of fruit in the recipe or add a bit of water, juice or soymilk to it and continue the straining process.

• What if my nutmilk is too thin? Try adding more nuts (as much as 1/4 cup) to the recipe. Or, add a bit of fruit (1/8 to 1/4 cup will often suffice). You could also experiment with guar gum   (1–2 tsp per recipe), which lends a soft and viscous texture to liquid. If you wish, guar gum can replace flaxseed in some recipes.

• What is the shelf life of a nutmilk and how can I keep it fresh? The shelf life varies, but I try to drink my recipes within 2-3 days. I use pure spring water (or water purified by carbon filter or reverse osmosis) to enhance the shelf life.

Recipes for Nut and Seed Milks

Essentially, one simple yet synergistically sound recipe can be adapted in many different ways to suit one's individual dietary needs and desires.

Almond Milks

Almonds are the browish, oval-shaped "stone" of the fruit of the almond tree, from the rose family, *Amygdalus communis*. They contain a balance of healthy proteins, fats, and carbohydrates as well as calcium, potassium, and magnesium.

Drinking nutmilks prepared with organic almond butter and almonds is one taste-pleasing way to support the health and development of teeth, bones, and muscles.

Pure and Sweet Almond Milk

1/2 c. organic raw almonds
1 Tbsp. fortified flaxseeds
1 tsp. lecithin granules
2 Tbsp. honey (or rice syrup)
1/8 tsp. almond extract
3 c. warm water

> *Prepare as indicated on Page 55:*
> **Nutmilks in Five Easy Steps**

Hints

You could add fruit to this nutmilk with tasty results, or other extracts of flavor.

Thought for Food

This nutmilk is simply delicious when served chilled. The pure almond flavor is so fresh. You will easily find a few ways to serve this milk or include it in recipes that call for milk.

Apple Ginger Almond Milk

1/3 c. organic raw almonds
1 Tbsp. fortified flaxseeds
1 tsp. lecithin granules
2/3 c. red organic apple (peeled and cut)
1/4 tsp. ginger powder (adjust if desired)
1/4 tsp. coconut extract
1 Tbsp. honey
2 Tbsp. rice syrup
3 c. hot water

> *Prepare as indicated on Page 55:*
> **Nutmilks in Five Easy Steps**

Hints

You may substitute honey with rice syrup, or vice versa. A hint more ginger powder than what is suggested will not overpower this drink. It is subtle as is.

Thought for Food

Served chilled, this nutmilk has a light and refreshing flavor. A rice cookie and a Japanese melody are all you need to complement it.

Banana Almondine Milk

1/3 c. organic raw almonds
1 Tbsp. fortified flaxseeds
1 tsp. lecithin granules
1 1/2 Tbsp. fresh almond butter
1/3 c. ripe banana
1 1/2 Tbsp. honey
1 Tbsp. sucanat
1/2–1 tsp. vanilla extract
3-3 1/4 c. almost-boiling water

> *Prepare as indicated on Page 55:*
> **Nutmilks in Five Easy Steps**

Hints

Sucanat (a powdered pure cane sugar juice) is available at
health food stores. Almond butter develops the creamier
calcium-rich taste of this milk. East Wind's organic
almond butter is a good choice. Rice milk could replace
part of the water, for variation.

Thought for Food

Bananas add the nutritional benefits of potassium and iron
to this beverage and are valuable in treating various
ailments such as stomach ulcers, colitis, diarrhea,
hemmorhoids, and general lack of energy. A treat served
hot or cold.

Banana Raisin Almond Milk

1/3 c. organic raw almonds
1 Tbsp. fortified flaxseeds
1 tsp. lecithin granules
1/8–1/4 c. dark raisins (soaked)
1/3 c. ripe banana
1 Tbsp. honey
1/2 tsp. vanilla extract
3 1/4 c. warm water
dash of barley malt sweetener powder
    (optional)

> *Prepare as indicated on Page 55:*
> **Nutmilks in Five Easy Steps**

Hints

Use a ripe banana (with brown speckled skin) for a well developed flavor. Raisins add the benefits of an iron-rich, strength-building food. Diluted coconut juice could replace water. Or, try rice milk.

Thought for Food

If you are weak or anemic or suffer from constipation, catarrh, or low blood pressure, this recipe provides an easy way to include iron-rich, strength-building foods in your diet. Banana raisin almond milk contains super nutrition. Consider it instant breakfast (in a glass) or serve with a piece of raisin toast or a tart.

Mellow Carob Cocoa Almond Milk

1/4 c. organic raw almonds
1/4 c. organic raw cashew nuts
1 Tbsp. fortified flaxseeds
1 tsp. lecithin granules
2 Tbsp. carob powder
1 tsp. cocoa powder
1/2 tsp. slippery elm powder
2 1/2 Tbsp. honey (adjust if desired)
1 tsp. vanilla extract
3 c. hot water

Prepare as indicated on Page 55:
Nutmilks in Five Easy Steps

Hints

Mixing a hint of cocoa with carob makes this taste like "authentic" hot chocolate. For variation: try ripe banana (1/2 c.) in addition to coconut extract. Vanilla soymilk could replace part of the water.

Thought for Food

Served warm, this is a cozy cup of nourishment in the winter after an outing to the skating rink.

Carob Orange Elm Tree Almond Milk

1/3 c. organic raw almonds
1 Tbsp. fortified flaxseeds
1 tsp. lecithin granules
1 Tbsp. carob powder
1/2 tsp. slippery elm powder
1/4 tsp. cinnamon powder
2 1/2 Tbsp. honey
1/2 tsp. orange extract
3 c. hot water
1/8 tsp. or pinch of anise (optional)

> Prepare as indicated on Page 55:
> **Nutmilks in Five Easy Steps**

Hints

I use Cook's Choice brand orange extract. The slippery elm powder always adds a nice healing quality to the drinks.

Thought for Food

This milk brings a conversational cup of flavor to time shared with someone special.

Mocha Mint Almond Milk

1/3 c. organic raw almonds
1 Tbsp. fortified flaxseeds
1 tsp. lecithin granules
2 Tbsp. carob powder
2 tsp. Cafix cereal grain beverage
       powder
2 1/2 Tbsp. honey
1/4 tsp. mint extract
3 c. hot water
dash of barley malt sweetener powder
       (optional)

> *Prepare as indicated on Page 55:*
> **Nutmilks in Five Easy Steps**

Hints

Stevia sweet leaf powder could replace a portion of the
sweetener in this milk, if desired. Soy milk could replace
part of the water.

Thought for Food

If you like the gourmet appeal of coffee and chocolate, this
mineral-rich drink will offer you a delicious caffeine-free
replacement.

Orange Fresh Almond Milk

1/3 c. organic raw almonds
1 Tbsp. fortified flaxseeds
1 tsp. lecithin granules
1/2 tsp. slippery elm powder
3 Tbsp. pure maple syrup
1/2 tsp. orange extract
3 c. hot water

> *Prepare as indicated on Page 55:*
> **Nutmilks in Five Easy Steps**

Hints

I use Cook's Choice brand orange extract.

Variation: Substitute maple with honey and replace elm powder with Cafix cereal beverage powder.

Thought for Food

Whichever way you serve this milk it is sure to be a taste pleaser!

Raspberry Almond-Butter Milk

1/3 c. organic raw almonds
1 Tbsp. fortified flaxseeds
1 tsp. lecithin granules
1 1/2 Tbsp. almond butter (roasted)
3 Tbsp. raspberry jelly
1 1/2 Tbsp. honey
1/2 tsp. vanilla extract
3-3 1/4 c. almost-boiling water

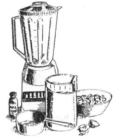

> *Prepare as indicated on Page 55:*
> **Nutmilks in Five Easy Steps**

Hints

The most delicious organic almond butter I've sampled is
one called Amandes de Jardin, imported from Jardine
Organic Ranch in Paso Robles, California. You may want
to use seedless raspberry jelly. Sorrel Ridge brand was used
in this drink.

Thought for Food

Almonds are notoriously rich in calcium, and this nutmilk
offers a smooth way to assimilate it.

Almond butter (with jelly) is a favorite with kids and
can substitute for peanut butter if one is allergic to it.

Cashew Milks

Golden cashew nuts are actually the embryo-shaped fruit of the tropical American Tree (*Anacardium occidentale* from the cashew family Anacardicae)

The savory cashew nut and nut butter are great body builders and easily digested when eaten raw. Organic cashew nuts make a nicely textured nutmilk and are a healthy source of calories, phosphorus, and calcium. If you want to increase your vitality or find nutritional ways to prevent teeth and gum problems, cashew milk will reward your efforts.

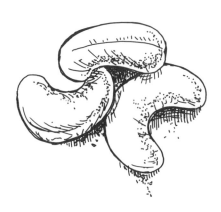

Golden Apricot Cashew Milk

1/2 c. organic raw cashew nuts and organic almonds (mix)
1 Tbsp. fortified flaxseeds
1 tsp. lecithin granules
1/4–1/3 c. dried (unsulphured) apricots
    (rehydrated)
2 1/2 Tbsp. honey
1 tsp. vanilla extract
1/4 tsp. orange extract
3 1/4–3 1/2 c. almost-boiling water
dash of barley malt sweetener powder or
pinch of sucanat (optional)

> *Prepare as indicated on Page 55:*
> **Nutmilks in Five Easy Steps**

Hints

Soak apricots overnight in dish of pure water, or pour almost boiling water over them and let stand for thirty minutes before blending.

Thought for Food

Apricots add the benefit of vitamin A, iron, calcium, and potassium, which makes them beneficial in cases of anemia, tuberculosis, and asthma. The golden fruit can also help with weight loss, toxemia, and blood impurities.

    The nourishing combination in this drink makes it a good before- or after-workout drink.

Blueberry Cashew Milk

1/3 c. organic raw cashews
1/8 c. almonds
1 Tbsp. fortified flaxseeds
1 tsp. lecithin granules
1/3 c. each, blueberries and banana
2 1/2 Tbsp. honey
1 tsp. vanilla extract
3 + c. almost-boiling water
1/2 c. coconut milk (optional)

> *Prepare as indicated on Page 55:*
> **Nutmilks in Five Easy Steps**

Hints

I blend sweet almonds and smooth textured cashews for
nutrition and flavor; a touch of coconut milk adds a
mellow fruitiness to the blueberries. Summer Song or
Lakewood brand coconut milk contain pear and grape
flavors.

Thought for Food

Blueberries are a natural blood cleanser. They have an
antiseptic value that is capable of soothing inflammation
in the intestines. They are also recommended for cases of
anemia, constipation, overweight conditions, and
complexion problems. If you like blueberries, this drink
should be especially pleasing.

Carob Butter Cashew Milk

1/3 c. organic raw cashew nuts
1 Tbsp. fortified flaxseeds
1 tsp. lecithin granules
1 Tbsp. carob powder
3/4 Tbsp. creamy peanut butter
2 Tbsp. honey
1 tsp. vanilla extract
3 1/4 c. almost-boiling water
dash of barley malt sweetener powder
    (optional)

Prepare as indicated on Page 55:
Nutmilks in Five Easy Steps

Hints

I use unsalted, nonhydrogenated, no-additive peanut
butter when available. It is easier to digest.

Thought for Food

Peanut butter is made from a bean *(legume)* although it is
often referred to as a nut butter. Its high-protein, high-fat
content make it desirable if you are underweight or have
low blood pressure.

    This milk is usually a hit with children since it
contains the flavors their bodies so often crave.

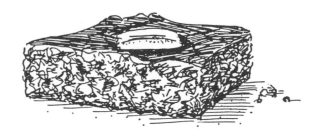

Lemon Coconut Cashew Milk

1/3 c. organic raw cashew nuts (or mix cashews with
        almonds or walnuts
1 Tbsp. fortified flaxseeds
1 tsp. lecithin granules
1/8 tsp. coconut extract
3 Tbsp. golden brown rice syrup
1/2 tsp. lemon extract
3 c. hot water
dash of barley malt sweetener powder
        (optional)

> *Prepare as indicated on Page 55:*
> **Nutmilks in Five Easy Steps**

Hints

A fine lemon extract, is Cook's Choice brand. Rice syrup (rather than honey) really makes a sweet difference in this recipe. Westbrae or Yinnies brand syrups are available at co-ops and health stores.

Thought for Food

Lemon coconut milk might just remind you of dessert in a glass!

Mock Eggnog Cashew Milk

1/3 c. organic raw cashew nuts (or mix cashews and almonds)
1 Tbsp. fortified flaxseeds
1 tsp. lecithin granules
3/4–1 tsp. grated lemon rind
Scant 1/2 tsp. nutmeg powder
2–3 Tbsp. honey
1 1/2 tsp. vanilla extract
3 c. almost-boiling water
dash of cinnamon
dash of barley malt sweetener powder or
     pinch of sucanat (optional)

Prepare as indicated on Page 55: **Nutmilks in Five Easy Steps**

Hints

I use unsprayed organic lemon rind.

Choose your vanilla extract with care to bring the best out of this nutmilk.

Thought for Food

Mock eggnog milk is a delicious way to make any day seem like a holiday. I like it best chilled.

Maple Sunshine Cashew Milk

1/3 c. organic raw cashew nuts
1 Tbsp. fortified flaxseeds
1 tsp. lecithin granules
1/2 tsp. slippery elm powder
2–3 Tbsp. pure maple syrup
1/4–1/2 tsp. orange extract
3 c. almost-boiling water

> *Prepare as indicated on Page 55:*
> **Nutmilks in Five Easy Steps**

Hints

Just a hint of orange extract is enough to let the flavor of "sunshine" through each sip.

Thought for Food

Served hot or cold, this luscious nutmilk offers a creamy, rich accompaniment to breakfasts and snacks. How about an orange-blossom muffin or an anise-flavored cookie with it?

Mellow Maple Cashew Milk

1/3 c. organic raw cashew nuts
1 Tbsp. fortified flaxseeds
1 tsp. lecithin granules
2 Tbsp. fresh creamy cashew butter
2 Tbsp. honey
1/2 tsp. maple extract
3 c. almost-boiling water
dash of barley malt sweetener powder or
         pinch of sucanat (optional)

> *Prepare as indicated on Page 55:*
> **Nutmilks in Five Easy Steps**

Hints

Cashew butter is available at natural food stores and well worth the shopping trip.

A fine maple extract is Cook's Choice brand.

Thought for Food

Maple cashew milk is a treat anytime, whether a la carte or in recipes (perhaps a pudding, frosting, or batter). You might even enjoy it as a nightcap.

Soft Peach Cashew Milk

1/3 c. organic raw cashew nuts (or mix cashew and
        almonds
1 Tbsp. fortified flaxseeds
1 tsp. lecithin granules
2 medium small fresh peeled peaches
2–3 Tbsp. honey
1/2 tsp. vanilla extract
1/8–1/4 tsp. orange extract
3 1/4 c. hot water
dash of barley malt sweetener powder
        (optional)

> *Prepare as indicated on Page 55:*
> **Nutmilks in Five Easy Steps**

Hints

I use ripe organic peaches to obtain the best flavor. A fine
brand of vanilla and orange extract is Cooks Choice.

Thought for Food

Peaches add the benefits of vitamins, minerals, and health
values useful in the treatment of anemia, a dull or spoiled
complexion, constipation, high blood pressure, bronchitis,
asthma, and toxicity of the body in general.

Soft peach milk is delightful when chilled, or serve
warm for a cool-weather breakfast drink.

Prairie Flower and Fruit Cashew Milk

1/3 c. organic raw cashew nuts
1 Tbsp. fortified flaxseeds
1 tsp. lecithin granules
1 medium red apple, peeled and sliced
2 Tbsp. honey
1/4–1/2 tsp. lemon extract
3 c. hot water

> *Prepare as indicated on Page 55:*
> **Nutmilks in Five Easy Steps**

Hints

A sweetish, organic apple is nice in this drink and attracts
the flavor of refreshing lemon. Cook's Choice brand lemon
extract is available at co-ops and health food stores.

Thought for Food

An apple adds the benefits of vitamins, minerals, and
cleansing values, which strengthen the blood and clear
away such conditions as constipation, catarrh, halitosis,
obesity, gallstones, intestinal toxins (poor digestion), and
complexion problems.

This milk has a fresh light taste and might be just the
thing to take the place of coffee or juice with your fruit
croissant.

Velvety Vanilla Cashew Milk

1/3 c. organic raw cashew nuts
1 Tbsp. fortified flaxseeds
1 tsp. lecithin granules
2 Tbsp. honey
1 1/2–2 tsp. vanilla extract
3 c. warm water
pinch of cinnamon or cardamom
        powder (optional)

> *Prepare as indicated on Page 55:*
> **Nutmilks in Five Easy Steps**

Hints

Whole, raw, organic cashews will insure the simple
elegance of this basic recipe as will a good quality vanilla.

Thought for Food

This vanilla milk is a delight on its own, or as a nondairy
base for recipes such as fruit smoothies, puddings, or
baked goods. It is also a fine topping for cereals (chilled)
and may be the simplest milk to make when you need a
quick beverage to go with a bar or cookie.

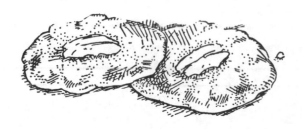

Pecan Milks

A botanical name associated with the tree-grown, butterscotch-colored pecan nut is *Hicoria*.

Fresh raw pecans have a luxuriously rich taste and are suppliers of calcium, phosphorus, potassium, and essential oils.

The pecan is valuable for the dietary treatment of low blood sugar and general weakness. It can also contribute to a healthy smile. Blended into nutmilks, pecans cannot help but contribute to your health.

Apple Fruit Harvest Pecan Milk

1/3 c. organic raw pecans
1 Tbsp. fortified flaxseeds
1 tsp. lecithin granules
1/3–2/3 c. dried (unsulphured) apples
    (rehydrated)
1/2 tsp. cinnamon powder
1/4 tsp. anise powder
2–3 Tbsp. golden brown rice syrup
3-1/2 c. hot water or very diluted apple juice
1 tsp.–1 Tbsp. of sucanat (optional)

> *Prepare as indicated on Page 55:*
> **Nutmilks in Five Easy Steps**

Hints

Sucanat—an unprocessed, powdered, pure cane sugar juice—is available at health food stores. The natural sweetness, vitamins, and minerals are condensed in dried apples and just a bit of soaking activates nutrients and flavor galore!

Thought for Food

I love this nutmilk, with its mellow rich nectary of dessertlike flavors. Rice syrup, cinnamon, and apples were made for each other! An apple tart, muffin, or croissant complement this milk.

Banana Cream Pecan Milk

1/3 c. organic raw pecans
1 Tbsp. fortified flaxseeds
1 tsp. lecithin granules
1/2 tsp. slippery elm powder
1/2–2/3 c. homemade dehydrated
    bananas (rehydrated)
2 Tbsp. maple or brown rice syrup
3-1/2 c. almost-boiling water
dash of spices, such as cinnamon and
    nutmeg

> *Prepare as indicated on Page 55:*
> **Nutmilks in Five Easy Steps**

Hints

An electric food dehydrator with cross airflow dries
bananas beautifully and is the secret to this creamy tasting
milk.

To Prepare: Peel ripe bananas. Find small dip in the
end of the fruit, gently press finger into end and split
banana in three long banana shaped segments. They are
dry when leathery yet pliable.

Thought for Food

The protein and carbohydrates in this milk are capable of
sustaining your energy for hours!

Caramel Date Pecan Milk

1/3 c. organic raw pecans
1 Tbsp. fortified flaxseeds
1 tsp. lecithin granules
1/3 c. barhi dates (pitted)
1 tsp. cashew butter and/or 1 tsp. soft
    butter
1 Tbsp. sucanat
1/8 tsp. butterscotch extract (adjust;
    optional)
1/2 tsp. vanilla extract
3 1/4 c. hot water

> *Prepare as indicated on Page 55:*
> **Nutmilks in Five Easy Steps**

Hints

Barhi dates are usually quite soft and do not require presoaking. They have a delicious caramel-like flavor

Thought for Food

This milk is so simple to make, yet so unique in ts appeal. Great with a butterscotch brownie!

Crescent Fruit Pecan Milk

1/3 c. organic raw pecans
1 Tbsp. fortified flaxseeds
1 tsp. lecithin granules
1/2 tsp. slippery elm powder
1/8 c. soaked dates
1/3 c. ripe banana
2 Tbsp. honey or sucanat
3 1/4 c. warm water
1/2 tsp. vanilla extract

> *Prepare as indicated on Page 55:*
> **Nutmilks in Five Easy Steps**

Hints

I use soft, pitted organic dates in this drink. Soak dates in
a bit of near-boiling water for fifteen minutes if you forgot
to rehydrate them overnight. Very diluted pear juice could
replace water.

Thought for Food

Bananas provide the body with iron and potassium. In
addition, their healing fibers can soothe ulcers, colitis, and
intestinal inflammation in general.

Sending the people you love to work or play, with this
drink in their bodies, will leave a good feeling in yours as
well.

Maple Pecan Milk

1/3 c. organic raw pecans
1 Tbsp. fortified flaxseeds
1 tsp. lecithin granules
1/2 tsp. slippery elm powder
3 Tbsp. pure maple syrup
1/2 tsp. vanilla extract
3 c. hot water
1/4 tsp. cinnamon (optional)
pinch of sucanat (optional)

> *Prepare as indicated on Page 55:*
> **Nutmilks in Five Easy Steps**

Hints

With its aromatic quality, highly nourishing slippery elm powder blends nicely with maple syrup. If desired, you can use less syrup, replacing it with a dash of barley malt sweetener powder and maple extract.

Thought for Food

This milk might just be the thing to serve with a pancake breakfast.

Pine Nut Milks

Pine nuts or "pinion nuts" as they are sometimes called, are the rather petite and pretty cream-colored seeds of any of several pine trees.

Digesting pine nuts raw, as in a nutmilk, provides the body with vitamins A and B in addition to calcium and iron.

Pine nuts are also rich in essential oils and healthy calories which make them desirable if you are an active person or need to build strength and energy.

Sunkissed Fruit and Pine Nut Milk

1/3–1/2 c. organic raw pine nuts (or mix with almonds)
1 Tbsp. fortified flaxseeds
1 tsp. lecithin granules
1/8–1/4 c. golden yellow raisins (soaked)
2–2 1/2 Tbsp. rice syrup or honey
1/8 tsp. orange extract
3-3 1/4 c. warm water

Prepare as indicated on Page 55:
Nutmilks in Five Easy Steps

Hints

Golden raisins add a slightly fruitier taste to this milk, especially with the addition of orange extract. Diluted apple cider could replace water.

Thought for Food

There is nothing like this nutritious kiss of flavor. You may never have tasted it before! Serve warm.

Ginger Sweet Pine Nut Milk

1/3 c. organic raw pine nuts
1 Tbsp. fortified flaxseeds
1 tsp. lecithin granules
1/4–1/2 tsp. ginger powder (adjust to taste)
1/8 tsp. cinnamon
1/8 tsp. allspice
1 1/2 Tbsp. light molasses
1 Tbsp. honey
1 Tbsp. sucanat
1/4 tsp. lemon extract
3 c. almost-boiling water
1 tsp. butter (optional)

> *Prepare as indicated on Page 55:*
> **Nutmilks in Five Easy Steps**

Hints

Lemon extract and ginger powder blend nicely in this rather unique tasting milk. You can serve it hot or chilled. I prefer it warmed.

Thought for Food

I prepared this milk one evening when I wanted to satisfy a dessert-craving for gingerbread. Serve warm.

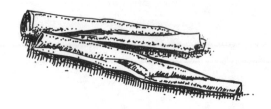

Peanut Butter and Strawberry Pine Nut Milk

1/3 c. organic raw pine nuts (or combine with almonds)
1 Tbsp. fortified flaxseeds
1 tsp. lecithin granules
1 1/2 Tbsp. organic peanut butter
2 1/2–3 Tbsp. organic strawberry
    conserves
1 Tbsp. honey (adjust as desired)
1/2–1 tsp. vanilla extract
3 1/4 c. almost-boiling water

> *Prepare as indicated on Page 55:*
> **Nutmilks in Five Easy Steps**

Hints

Smooth style peanut butter works best for blending this milk. I use Cascadia Farm brand jelly available at food co-ops and health food stores.

Thought for Food

Kids will guess the flavors in this after a couple of tasty sips. I sure like the idea of preparing food with organic ingredients!

Sweet Pear and Pine Nut Milk

1/3 c. organic raw pine nuts (or combine with almonds)
1 Tbsp. fortified flaxseeds
1 tsp. lecithin granules
1/3 c. dried (unsulphured) pears
      (rehydrated)
2 tsp. carob powder
2 1/2 Tbsp. honey
1/8–1/4 tsp. mint extract
3 1/2 c. almost-boiling water
dash of cinnamon

> *Prepare as indicated on Page 55:*
> **Nutmilks in Five Easy Steps**

Hints

Soak pears in almost boiling water for 1/2 hour before blending, or soak overnight. You could substitute part of the honey with barley malt sweetener powder.

Thought for Food

Mineral-rich dried pears and carob powder make this a nutritious choice!

Creamy Pineapple Pine Nut Milk

1/3 c. organic raw pine nuts
1 Tbsp. fortified flaxseeds
1 tsp. lecithin granules
1/2 c. crushed pineapple
1/4 c. ripe banana, mashed
2 Tbsp. organic brown rice syrup
1 Tbsp. honey
1/4–1/2 tsp. orange extract
1/4 tsp. vanilla extract
3 1/4-3 1/3 c. almost boiling water

> *Prepare as indicated on Page 55:*
> **Nutmilks in Five Easy Steps**

Hints

I used canned pineapple (crushed in its own juice), for this milk, but if you have a sweet, fresh pineapple, you could use it instead.

Remember to be absolutely certain your pine nuts are fresh (refrigerated always).

Thought for Food

This milk, with its potassium, magnesium and mineral-rich banana content and its enzyme-rich pineapple juice, is nutritious and easy to digest. Serve it chilled to flatter the taste of each ingredient.

Walnut Milks

Walnuts are the nuts from trees of the genus *Juglans*. Abundant in vitamins, minerals, and essential oils, walnuts are helpful in alleviating constipation and liver ailments, and they strengthen the muscles. Combined with other nutritious delicious ingredients, the benefits of walnuts are simply multiplied.

Banana Coconut Cream Walnut Milk

1/3 c. organic raw walnuts
1 Tbsp. fortified flaxseeds
1 tsp. lecithin granules
2/3 c. ripe banana (mashed)
2 Tbsp. honey
1 Tbsp. rice syrup
1/2 tsp. coconut extract
1/2 tsp. vanilla extract
3 c. hot water (or try coconut milk or vanilla soymilk)

> *Prepare as indicated on Page 55:*
> **Nutmilks in Five Easy Steps**

Hints

You could use either all honey for sweetening or all rice syrup, depending upon your preference.

Thought for Food

I served this pleasant nutmilk flavor combination to a rather finicky child whose palate was developed on cows milk, and he has never stopped asking me to "make it again."

Blackberry Banana Walnut Milk

1/3 c. organic raw walnuts
1 Tbsp. fortified flaxseeds
1 tsp. lecithin granules
1/8 c. blackberries
2/3 c. ripe banana (mashed)
1 tsp. almond butter
1/8 tsp. cinnamon
2 1/2–3 Tbsp. honey
3 1/4–3 1/2 c. hot water

> *Prepare as Indicated on Page 57:*
> **Nutmilks in Four Easy Steps**

Hints

I use frozen blackberries in this milk. You will find they add a bit of tangy flavor and purplish color.

A dash of carob or slippery elm could also be added.

Thought for Food

This milk is uncharacteristic of my other nutmilks, but tasty just the same, especially if chilled. Drink it all by itself for quick nourishment, or try using it as a nondairy base blended with a frozen banana to make a "smoothie"!

Coconut Date and Walnut Milk

1/3 c. organic raw walnuts
1 Tbsp. fortified flaxseeds
1 tsp. lecithin granules
1/3 c. soaked chopped dates
1 Tbsp. rice syrup or honey (adjust as
    desired)
1 1/2 tsp. vanilla extract
1/4 tsp. orange extract or 1/4 tsp.
    coconut extract
3 1/3 c. almost-boiling water

> *Prepare as indicated on Page 55:*
> **Nutmilks in Five Easy Steps**

Hints

Try substituting a portion of water in this recipe with coconut milk, vanilla soymilk or rice milk.

Thought for Food

Dates are a concentrated, yet nourishing carbohydrate food and are easily digested. They have been found valuable in the nutritional treatment of anemia, low blood pressure, ulcers, colitis, tuberculosis, and nervous and respiratory conditions. Drink to your health!

Fruit Jewel and Carob Walnut Milk

1/3 c. organic raw walnuts
1 Tbsp. fortified flaxseeds
1 tsp. lecithin granules
1 Tbsp. creamy sesame tahini nut butter
1/4 c. soaked medjhool dates or raisins
1 small red apple (peeled and sliced)
2 Tbsp. carob
2 1/2 Tbsp. honey (adjust as desired)
3 1/3 c. hot water
1/2 tsp. vanilla (optional)

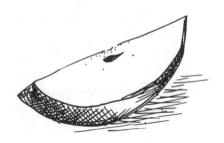

> *Prepare as indicated on Page 55:*
> **Nutmilks in Five Easy Steps**

Hints

Use a sweet (rather than tart) apple for this drink.

Variation: Omit apple and/or dates and add 1/3 to 1/2 c. ripe banana with vanilla flavoring to taste.

Thought for Food

Every ingredient in this drink carries nutritional weight.

Pumpkinseed Milks

Crunchy, earthen-green pumpkin seeds come to us in bountiful supply from the mothering pumpkin vine known as *Cucurbita Pepo*. Pumpkin seeds contain nutrients such as phosphorus, iron, calcium, and vitamin A, as well as nutritional factors that nourish the prostate gland and aid in male hormone production. Females should not pass these seeds by, however, since they are also reliable body builders and intestinal regulators.

Minty Carob Pumpkinseed Milk

1/2 c. organic pumpkin seeds (or mix with almonds)
1 Tbsp. fortified flaxseeds
1 tsp. lecithin granules
2 Tbsp. carob powder
2 Tbsp. honey
1/4 tsp. mint extract
3 c. hot water
dash of barley malt sweetener powder
    (optional)

> *Prepare as indicated on Page 55:*
> **Nutmilks in Five Easy Steps**

Hints

You could substitute part of the water in this recipe with vanilla soymilk for delicious creaminess.

Stevia sweet leaf powder may also be used to sweeten this drink. Cocoa powder could replace part of the carob.

Thought for Food

Minty carob pumpkinseed milk has a refreshing taste, chilled or hot. A scoop of ice cream in the hot version creates an instant dessert drink you may want to share with a friend.

Chocolate Mountain Pumpkinseed Milk

1/3 c. organic raw pumpkinseeds
1 Tbsp. fortified flaxseeds
1 tsp. lecithin granules
2 1/2–3 Tbsp. fruit-sweetened chocolate
    sauce
1 Tbsp. honey
1 tsp. vanilla extract
1/8 tsp. mint extract
3 c. hot water

> *Prepare as indicated on Page 55:*
> **Nutmilks in Five Easy Steps**

Hints

A delightfully healthful brand of chocolate sauce containing pineapple juice, unsweetened Dutch cocoa, concentrated pear and peach juices, and pure vanilla is Chocolate Mountain Brand, distributed by Barbara's Bakery from California. Malted vanilla soymilk could replace part of the water.

Thought for Food

This nutmilk is rich and yummy and less apt to produce the guilt that an artificially embalmed chocolate dairy milk might.

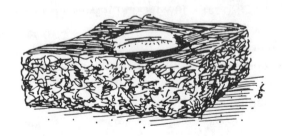

Sweet Fruit-of-the-Vine Pumpkinseed Milk

1/3-1/2 c. organic raw pumpkin seeds (or mix with almonds)
1 Tbsp. fortified flaxseeds
1 tsp. lecithin granules
1/3 c. pureed pumpkin
2–3 Tbsp. honey (vary with sweetener below*)
1 tsp. cinnamon
1/4 tsp. anise (adjust as desired)
1 1/2 tsp. vanilla extract
3 1/3 c. warm water (or try rice milk or soy milk)
*dash of Dr. Bronners barley malt
  sweetener powder or pinch of
  sucanat (optional)

> *Prepare as indicated on Page 55:*
> **Nutmilks in Five Easy Steps**

Hints

I use canned pumpkin in this recipe unless I have autumn leftovers on hand. Sucanat is extra tasty in this beverage.

Thought for Food

Pumpkin contains lots of vitamin A and potassium as well as healthy carbohydrates. The yellow fruit is capable of nourishing the spleen and will soothe inflamed intestines, stomach ulcers, and hemorrhoids. According to nutritionists, it can also raise low blood pressure and carry nourishment to the body.

If you like spices, you will like this nutmilk. Enjoy with a pumpkin cookie or bar, or consider it a high-protein breakfast drink (chilled). Served warm, it makes one appreciate seasonable garden tidings.

Rice Nectar Pumpkinseed Milk

1/3 c. organic raw pumpkinseeds
1 Tbsp. fortified flaxseeds
1 tsp. lecithin granules
1/2 c. ripe banana (mashed)
1/4 tsp. cardamom
3 Tbsp. organic brown rice syrup
1 tsp. vanilla extract
3 c. warm water

> *Prepare as indicated on Page 55:*
> **Nutmilks in Five Easy Steps**

Hints

I used golden-blonde-colored rice syrup in this milk (made by Lundberg Farms). It has a mellow sweetness (not as concentrated as honey) and nicely enhances the banana's sweet nourishment.

Thought for Food

The little bit of spice in this nutmilk lends it a rich touch of flavor. Serve it warmed (as a nightcap) or chilled anytime you crave something good for you!

Sesame Seed Milks

Sesame seeds are derived from an East Indian herb also known as *gama grass*.

Sesame seeds and sesame butter are richly abundant in calcium and contain a share of potassium, phosphorus, and vitamin E.

The vitamin E content in the seeds is said to strengthen the heart, liver, and nerves. If you suffer with constipation, an underweight condition, or have undesireable local swellings or tumors, sesame seeds can offer nutritional help. They are also extremely beneficial for lactating women when the body's demand for calcium is particularly high.

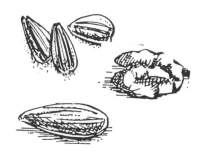

Clover Honey and Sesame Seed Milk

1/3 c. organic raw cashew nut or almonds
1 Tbsp. fortified flaxseeds
1 1/2 Tbsp. sesame tahini nut butter
3 Tbsp. honey
2 tsp. vanilla extract
3-3 1/4 c. almost-boiling water

> *Prepare as indicated on Page 55:*
> **Nutmilks in Five Easy Steps**

Hints

I use a light rather than dark honey for a greater emphasis on the sesame.

Thought for Food

The simple flavors come through in this milk, as does its nourishing calcium content.

Creamy Sesame and Sunflower Seed Milk

1/3 c. organic raw sunflower seeds
1 Tbsp. fortified flaxseeds
1 tsp. lecithin granules
2–3 tsp. sesame tahini nut butter
1/3 c. ripe banana (mashed)
2– 2 1/2 Tbsp. honey or rice syrup
1 tsp. vanilla extract
3 1/4–3 1/3 c. warm water

> *Prepare as indicated on Page 55:*
> **Nutmilks in Five Easy Steps**

Hints

I use Arrowhead Mills brand organic sesame tahini in this milk. Diluted cider or pear juice can replace water.

Thought for Food

Sunflower and sesame are the "King" and "Queen" of nourishing seeds. You will be able to taste and feel their virtues.

Raisin Valencia Nut and Sesame Seed Milk

1/3 c. organic raw sunflower seeds
1 Tbsp. fortified flaxseeds
1 tsp. lecithin granules
1 tsp. sesame tahini nut butter
1 tsp. smooth organic peanut butter
1 1/2 Tbsp. honey (adjust as desired)
2 Tbsp. raisins (soaked)
1/8 c. (small chunk) of ripe banana
1 1/2 tsp. vanilla extract
3 1/4 c. almost-boiling water
dash of barley malt sweetener powder
        (optional)

> *Prepare as indicated on Page 55:*
> **Nutmilks in Five Easy Steps**

Hints

You can add more raisins to this recipe if desired. A pinch of coriander (ground spice) is also an option.

Thought for Food

You can use this milk in a recipe for baked goods, or kids might like it served cold with peanut butter sandwiches.

Sunflower Seed Milks

Sunflower seeds—those small, greyish edible gems that peek out from the flowering heads of the tall, proud summertime plant of the genus *Helianthus*—are a wonderfully balanced whole food.

Raw, organically grown seeds ought to be a part of everyone's diet (especially vegetarians) since they nourish the entire body. Their near-complete protein content, plus vitamins and minerals, provide the body with many nutrients needed for growth and repair. If you suffer with weak eyes, poor fingernails, tooth decay, lackluster skin and hair, or arthritis, sunflower seed milk on your menus can pleasantly help to change these conditions within a very short time.

Cinnamon Spiced Sunflower Seed Milk

1/2 c. organic raw sunflower seeds
1 Tbsp. fortified flaxseeds
1 tsp. lecithin granules
2 Tbsp. honey
1/4 tsp. cinnamon
1 tsp. vanilla extract
3 c. hot water
dash of barley malt sweetener powder or
      pinch of sucanat (optional)

> *Prepare as indicated on Page 55:*
> **Nutmilks in Five Easy Steps**

Hints

For a roasted version of this drink, try using fresh, unsalted, toasted sunflower seeds and add 2 teaspoons carob powder.

Thought for Food

This sunflower seed milk has a distinctive "earthy" taste and sweet nutritive value.

    Sunflower seed nutmilks are best when served within twenty-four to forty-eight hours.

Golden Minerals Sunflower Seed Milk

1/3 c. organic raw sunflower seeds
1 Tbsp. fortified flaxseeds
1 tsp. lecithin granules
1 Tbsp. light Barbados molasses
1 tsp. carob powder
1/3 c. ripe banana (mashed)
2 Tbsp. honey
1/2–1 tsp. vanilla extract
3–3 1/4 c. almost-boiling water

> Prepare as indicated on Page 55:
> **Nutmilks in Five Easy Steps**

Hints

Be sure to use light rather than dark molasses.

Thought for Food

This sunflower milk has plenty of the calcium and iron everybody needs. You could cool down a creamy bowl of hot cereal with it.

High Protein Sunflower Seed Sprout Milk

1/3 c. 12+ hour sunflower seed sprouts
1/3 c. organic raw sunflower seeds
1 Tbsp. fortified flaxseeds
1 tsp. lecithin granules
2 1/2 Tbsp. honey
1 1/2 tsp. vanilla extract
1/2 c. banana (optional)
3 1/4—3 1/3 c. warm water (or rice milk)

> *Prepare as indicated on Page 55:*
> **Nutmilks in Five Easy Steps**

Hints

Sprouting sunflower seeds increases their vitamin and enzyme content a hundred fold!

To Sprout: Thoroughly rinse and drain 1 c. sunflower seeds. Put into a small (16 oz.) earthen bowl or Tupperware container. Cover seeds with pure water; add two inches more water. Let seeds absorb water for twelve hours or more. Seeds will become crunchier (more "raw") and begin to bud a *tiny* tail half the length of the seed itself. Rinse and drain before using in recipe.

Thought for Food

This highly nourishing milk has a desirable live food taste. It is rather perishable, however, so drink it immediately or within twelve hours of preparation to obtain the best flavor and value.

Using Nutmilks in Recipes

Baked Goods

Nut milks can be stirred into your favorite cake recipe for moist texture and flavor. Some of the nut milks you may want to try for this purpose include: "Banana Coconut Walnut," "Lemon Coconut Cashew/Walnut," "Banana Raisin Almond," "Carob Orange Almond," "Maple Pecan" or "Orange Fresh Almond" milks.

Breakfast Cereal

Nutmilks, chilled or warmed, can be poured over hot creamy breakfast cereals for a super nourishing meal. For this purpose, you may want to try "Cinnamon Spiced Sunflower Seed," "Apple Fruit Harvest Pecan" and "Banana Raisin Almond" milks. For dry cereal, use a thinner version of nutmilk such as "Sweet Almond" milk, or try blending a banana or raisin-flavored nutmilk with soy or rice milk.

Blender Drinks

Nut milks are perfect for blending smoothies and shakes. (See my book *Super Smoothies: Taste the Nectar of Life!*) Plain, thin-textured nut milks such as "Velvety Vanilla Cashew" or "Pure and Sweet Almond" milk mix well with frozen fruits. Creamy nutmilks such as "Apple Fruit Harvest Pecan" milk could be blended with fresh or frozen strawberries for an extra luscious and creamy treat. Or, you could try "Creamy Banana Coconut Walnut" milk or "Banana Raisin Almond" milk blended with frozen bananas. Yum!

Brunch

A reader of mine once wrote to me that he used my "Orange Fresh Almond" milk in a batch of scrambled eggs and that they were the best eggs he had ever eaten! Now, that is a recipe idea I never would have thought of on my own.

My favorite nutmilk recipes to serve at a brunch include: "Banana Coconut Walnut," "Apple Fruit Harvest Pecan," "Orange Apricot Almond/Cashew" and "Mocha Mint Almond," to name a few. Nutmilks are the perfect accompaniment to muffins and croissants.

Snacks and Dessert Drinks

Nutmilks can be used to make pudding if you blend them with arrowroot powder or cornstarch and stir over high heat until thickened. For this purpose try: "Mellow Carob Almond," "Banana Raisin Almond," "Chocolate Mountain Pumpkin Seed," "Fruit-of-the-Vine Pumpkin Seed," "Coconut Date Walnut," "Caramel Date Pecan," "Banana Cream Pecan" and "Lemon Coconut Walnut" Recipes may need additional flavoring extracts or sweeteners.

Nut milks can be enjoyed on their own or served with a muffin, cookie or bar for snacks. Children love the warm version of "Mello Carob Cocoa Almond" milk because it reminds them of hot cocoa.

Nut milks make a nice nite-cap, especially when served warm. Soothing flavors might include: "Rice Nectar Pumpkin seed," "Fruit of the Vine Pumpkin Seed," "Mock Eggnog Cashew," "Ginger Sweet Pine Nut, "Mellow Carob Cocoa Almond," "Banana Coconut Walnut," and "Banana Almondine."

Be Creative!

Directory of Nutmilk Ingredient Suppliers

Most natural food cooperatives and health food stores stock the ingredients found in the recipes. The following distributors supply those retailers. Their mail order catalogs are available for anyone's convenience and you may order certain items direct from the company itself if necessary.

Nuts, Seeds, and Dried Fruit

Jaffe Bros.
28560 Hilac Road
P.O. Box 636
Valley Center, California 92080
(617) 749-1133

Mail order; dried fruits, oils, nuts, seeds, carob powder, etc.

Walnut Acres
Penns Creek, PA 17862
(717) 837-0601

Mail order; high quality; no preservatives, rain forest nuts, organic sunflower seeds and preserves.

Erewhon Inc.
236 Washington Street
Brookline, Massachusetts 02146
(800) 222-8028

Mail order; nuts and nut butters, seeds, etc.

K. B. Hall Ranch
11999 Ojai S.P. Road
Ojai, California 93025
(805) 646-4512

Mail order; preservative free dried apricots and walnuts.

International Protein Industries, Inc.
P.O. Box 871
Smithtown, New York 11787

Chemical free hulled sesame seeds.

Ahlers Organic Date and Grapefruit Garden
P.O. Box 726
Mecca, California 92254
(619) 396-2337

Mail order; organically grown dates.

Horizon Natural Products
Soquel, California 95073

Stevia Sweet Leaf Powder

Now Foods
Villa Park, Illinois 60181

Stevia Sweet Leaf Powder.

Es Condido
Box 28
California 92025

Dr. Bronner's Barley Malt & Calcium Malt Powder.

Juices and Fruit Preserves

Sorrell Ridge Farm
100 Markley Street
Port Reading, New Jersey 07064
(201) 636-2060

Fruit conserves.

Heinke
5365 Clark Road
Paradise, California 95969-6399
(916) 877-4847

Feature: fresh fruit juices with no sweeteners added.

Special Extras

Red Saffron Herbs
3009 16th Avenue South
Minneapolis, Minnesota 55407

Feature: bee pollen and spices and slippery elm powder.

American Health Products
El Molino Foods
Ramsey, New Jersey 07446

Carob powder.

Arrowhead Mills
P.O. Box 866
Hereford, Texas 79045
(806) 364-0730

Organically raised flaxseed, whole unground.

Omega Life Inc.

Flaxseed; ground to powder and combined with nutritional cofactors.

Fruitful Yield
4950 W. Oakton
Skokie, Illinois
(312) 679-8975

Feature; guargum (a substitute for flaxseed if desired).

Flavoring Extracts

Cook Flavoring Co.
Cook's Choice Extracts
P.O. Box 890
Tacoma, Washington 98401
(206) 627-5499

Mail order; retail flavoring extracts
in a high quality array of flavors.

Frontier Cooperative Herbs
Box 69
Norway, Iowa 52318

25 natural flavors, all natural, no
alcohol or preservatives.

Natural Sweeteners

Lundberg Farms
Richvale, California
95974-0369

Organic Brown Rice Syrup.

Spring Tree Corporation
P.O. Box 1160
Brattleboro, Vermont 05301
(802) 254-8784

Mail order; organic maple syrup &
carob powder.